In All Seasons
For All Reasons

In All Seasons, For All Reasons

Praying Throughout the Year

James Martin, SJ

A *Give Us This Day* Book

LITURGICAL PRESS

Collegeville, Minnesota

www.litpress.org

A *Give Us This Day* Book
published by Liturgical Press

Cover design by Ann Blattner

1   2   3   4   5   6   7   8   9

Library of Congress Cataloging-in-Publication Data

Names: Martin, James, 1960– author.
Title: In all seasons, for all reasons : praying throughout the year / James Martin, SJ.
Description: Collegeville, Minnesota : Liturgical Press, 2017. | "A Give Us This Day book."
Identifiers: LCCN 2017020634 (print) | LCCN 2017008795 (ebook) | ISBN 9780814645314 (ebook) | ISBN 9780814645079
Subjects: LCSH: Prayer—Christianity. | Catholic Church—Doctrines.
Classification: LCC BV210.3 (print) | LCC BV210.3 .M365 2017 (ebook) | DDC 248.3/2—dc23
LC record available at https://lccn.loc.gov/2017020634

A Rich Tradition

For All Reasons

In All Seasons

Teach Us to Pray: An Introduction

One day, according to the Gospel of Luke, Jesus' disciples caught sight of their teacher praying. "Lord, teach us to pray," they said (Lk 11:1).

This vignette shows us not only Jesus' prayerful life, but what must have been the powerful appeal of what he was doing. It's something like a child seeing a friend engaged in something enjoyable, like skipping rope, and saying, "Show me how to do that!"

Jesus responded by teaching his friends the Our Father, often called the "perfect prayer." But even afterward, his followers probably continued to wonder about what it meant to pray.

Even for those who know the Our Father, the disciples' request remains a timeless one. Many Catholics, indeed many believers, doubt that they pray the "right" way. In this collection of brief essays drawn from my monthly column in *Give Us This Day*, together we will explore many ways to pray—in all seasons and for all reasons.

What is the "right" way to pray? The Rosary? Adoration of the Blessed Sacrament? Reading Scripture? Imaginative prayer? Well, as far as I'm concerned, the right way is whatever works best for you in your particular time and place. For God meets you where you are. And the fact that you are holding this book in your hand means you are already open to that encounter.

Like the disciples, we continue to ask God to teach us to pray, trusting that we will be answered in ways that will help us, move us—and even surprise us.

James Martin, SJ
New York City

11

**A Rich
Tradition**

Praying the Our Father

Lord, teach us to pray" (Luke 11:1). It is the simple request of a disciple who wants to learn from his Master. John the Baptist, it seems, had taught his disciples to pray. And Jesus' followers had seen him "withdraw" to pray, many times. Indeed, Jesus prays so frequently in Luke's Gospel it is sometimes called the "Gospel of Prayer." And Jesus is happy to teach his disciples: "When you pray, say 'Father, hallowed be your name.' "

One of the most surprising aspects of the Our Father is that much of it is petitionary. I mention this because petitionary prayer sometimes gets a bad rap in spiritual circles. Many people have told me that they feel they shouldn't ask for things in prayer: it's too selfish, they say.

Yet Jesus asks us to ask. He is confident before the Father in prayer, and he encourages us to ask for what we need: our daily bread, of course, but also deliverance from evil and temptation.

And whom are we asking? Not some far-off, impersonal God, but our Father. Now, the very word "Father" can be difficult for some people. Some have, or had, fathers who were cruel, judgmental, or even abusive. Also, the language can seem sexist—after all, God has no gender. But Jesus' father is the tenderhearted *Abba*, an Aramaic word roughly translated as "Dad." A few years ago in Jerusalem, I saw a young girl running to catch up with her father, shouting, "Abba! Abba!" It is to this loving parent that we turn when we pray the Our Father.

So ask away, and remember that you're asking your *Abba*.

Praying the Hail Mary

The first prayer I learned as a boy was the Hail Mary. (Don't ask me why it wasn't the Our Father: maybe it had something to do with not attending a Catholic school!) Sometimes when I wanted help from God, I would pray the Hail Mary on the way to school, my feet hitting the sidewalk in sync with the prayer's cadence: "*Hail* Mary, *full* of grace, the *Lord* is with thee . . ."

Mainly I used the prayer as a kind of "payment" for what I wanted from God. The bigger the favor from God, the more Hail Marys I would say.

Not until I was a Jesuit novice was I able to appreciate the underlying beauty of the prayer, and was able to see it as a twofold prayer, of Scripture and tradition. The first part of the prayer is taken almost directly from the greeting of the angel Gabriel to Mary in the Gospel of Luke. The second part of the prayer is a brief compendium of Marian tradition, which invokes one of her traditional titles, "Mother of God," and asks for her prayers.

Some of us (myself included) recite the Hail Mary almost as if in a trance—for example, when we say the Rosary—perhaps without pausing to reflect on the beauty of the individual words. But that's okay, as long as this ancient prayer reminds us that we are asking for the aid of someone who has long been listening to human hopes and desires.

Whether we are a child asking for help at school or a sick or elderly person "at the hour of our death," Mary hears our prayer. And prays for us.

Praying the Rosary

The Rosary, one of the oldest forms of Catholic prayer, has been a popular devotion in the Catholic Church since roughly the fifteenth century. Originally this circlet of beads enabled laypeople to pray along with monastic communities. (The 150 individual prayers mirror the 150 psalms. There are 10 Hail Marys in each "decade" of the Rosary, and there are five decades each for the sorrowful, joyful, and glorious "mysteries." That is: 10 x 5 x 3 = 150.)

Briefly put, one begins the Rosary with the Apostles' Creed, and then prays a Hail Mary for each of the small beads and an Our Father for each of the larger ones. Along the way, one meditates on various events (mysteries) in the lives of Mary and Jesus.

Such rote or repetitive prayers are sometimes dismissed by "sophisticated" Catholics. Yet believers can use the Rosary in many ways: slowly meditating on the words of the beautiful prayers, pondering the lives of Mary and Jesus (one person described the Rosary as "Mary's photo album"), or using the rote prayers as a mantra to quiet oneself in order to enter more deeply into God's presence. For me, the Rosary helps when it's hard to concentrate, and the familiar prayers I've known since childhood are an unfailing comfort.

As an elderly woman once told her Jesuit son, "When I pray the Rosary, I look at God, and God looks at me."

Mary as Patron and Companion

Most Catholics are familiar with Marian devotions, especially the Rosary—even if some may misunderstand these practices.

Though Mary without question holds a most special place in the roster of saints, it is important to remember that we don't worship Mary, and we don't see her as equal to God. We venerate her under many titles: *Mother of God, Our Lady, The Blessed Mother,* among others. But worship is reserved for God. When we ask for Mary's help as a patron (someone who prays for us) we believe that she is praying *to God.*

Mary's entire life was in service to God. "Behold, I am the handmaid of the Lord," she says to the angel Gabriel (Luke 1:38). And her last words in Scripture point to Jesus when at the Wedding at Cana she says, "Do whatever he tells you" (John 2:5). In all this she is a model of fidelity and prayer.

But the saints are not just our patrons; they are our companions. Seeing Mary as our companion means remembering that the Blessed Mother was once Miriam of Nazareth, a poor woman in an insignificant village. God chose one of the most marginal of people—indigent, young, unmarried, living in an occupied region under Roman rule—to be the mother of Jesus. She knows what it means to live on the edge. Mary dealt with surprises in life, knew suffering, and rejoiced over God's activity.

In a word, Mary was human.

So the next time you take out a rosary or say a Marian prayer like the *Memorare,* remember that it unites us not only with Our Lady enthroned in heaven but also with Miriam of Nazareth.

Praying with the Saints

The saints help us in two main ways: as *companions* and *patrons*. As companions, they offer us examples of how to lead Christian lives. But they do so in particular ways.

St. Peter was different from St. Francis of Assisi, who was in turn different from St. Thérèse of Lisieux. Each saint was holy in his or her own way, and their individual lives show us that we can be holy in *our* own ways.

Being a saint means being yourself—nothing more, but more important, nothing less.

The saints are also our patrons, the ones who pray for us. Some people misunderstand this aspect of Catholicism, believing that Catholics "worship" the saints, as if they were God. Of course the saints are not God—and they would be the first to tell you this! Some people also mistakenly think Catholics believe saints "answer" prayers. No, God does this. Saints simply pray for us in heaven, much as a friend on earth would pray for us. This is one way to pray with the saints—by asking for their "intercession."

We can also pray with the saints by reading their writings, meditating on their lives and, finally, by following their examples—helping the poor, living a prayerful life, and exercising charity.

In this way, their roles as patron and companion are joined, and we find ourselves slowly becoming saints in our own lives.

Examination of Conscience

St. Ignatius Loyola used to say there was one prayer that his brother Jesuits should never miss praying daily (other than the Mass). Not the Rosary, or the *Memorare*, or the *Anima Christi*, as wonderful as those prayers are, but another one: the examination of conscience.

Why? Because the examination of conscience, a prayerful review of the day, helps us to see where God is at work in our lives. And Ignatius knew that when we stop noticing this we start to feel distant from God. Moreover, since God communicates with us in our daily lives, we need to pay attention to what God is saying.

Essentially, Ignatius's examination of conscience (also known as the "examination of consciousness" or by its Spanish name, the *examen*) has five steps. First, remind yourself you're in God's presence. Second, call to mind anything for which you're grateful, then savor it and give thanks. Third, review the entire day, from start to finish, noticing places of encounter with God—whether in work, family life, friendships, nature, reading . . . or anything. Ask yourself: in this moment, did I accept God's invitation? Fourth, ask God for forgiveness for your sins. And fifth, ask God for the grace needed for the next day.

Many of us are quite busy. So while we say we *know* God is with us day to day, we often don't pause to notice. And not noticing is like neglecting to acknowledge a favor a friend has done for us. Noticing, as we do in the examination of conscience, helps us deepen our gratitude for God's grace, which in turn strengthens our faith.

Lectio Divina

The phrase conjures up images of wizened monks bent over ancient Bibles. But *lectio divina* (Latin for "sacred reading") is a form of prayer accessible not only to modern-day monks but to all contemporary believers. It is, simply, a way of encountering God in Scripture, a way of sitting with the text and listening.

For many Catholics, the Bible can seem daunting. Daniel J. Harrington, SJ, the New Testament scholar, used to tell the story of a Bible salesman coming to his family's house when Dan was seven. "Sorry," said his mother to the salesman. "We're Catholics. We don't read the Bible."

But since the Second Vatican Council, Catholics have been encouraged not only to read the Bible, but pray with it. And the ancient practice of *lectio divina* is a marvelous way to engage the text. I'll use Father Harrington's four easy steps for *lectio*, which take the form of prayerful questions: *First*, ask, "What does the text say?" What is going on? *Second*, "What does the text say to me?" Here, we ask what relevance the passage has for our daily lives. *Third*, "What do I want to say to God about this text?" Now, we begin an honest conversation with God. *Fourth*, "What difference will this text make in my life?" Encountering the Bible always means conversion and transformation, if we are open to it.

The Bible is the Living Word of God. The Holy Spirit breathes through it. That's one reason you can return to the most familiar of passages and find surprises. Remember that as you read the Old and New Testaments, God will be helping you pray. God wants to be found. It is God, in fact, who is opening up the text for you.

Resting on a Word

People often grow frustrated when nothing seems to be "happening" in their prayer. It's a natural reaction. Most of us like to get things "done." Most of us like to see results after we've spent an hour, or even a few minutes, in prayer.

Occasionally, the desire for results can lead us to rush through prayer—as if it's just another task to be completed. It would be as if we were spending time with a friend and kept wondering, "What am I *getting* out of this?" Prayer is more about the relationship than the results.

One way to slow ourselves down is by resting on a single word. Take a favorite passage of Scripture, or the reading of the day, and rather than trying to digest the entire reading, allow God to draw you toward one word. And trust that God is at work in your attraction to that word.

Take Psalm 139 as an example. It begins: "O God you have searched me and known me." You may find yourself drawn to the word "known." Now just rest there quietly and see where that might lead. Perhaps you've never thought about God knowing you—knowing your desires, your fears, your hopes. Maybe you realize that you'd like to start telling God more about your life, so that you can feel better known by God. Or perhaps you just want to sit with the word and savor it. Sometimes resting happens in ways that move beyond words.

As an antidote to "results-oriented" prayer, try resting on a single word. And, through this, allow God to rest in you.

Resting in God

A few years ago I told my spiritual director I was disappointed with my recent prayer life. Why? Because nothing much seemed to be happening. "All I do is rest in God's presence," I said. He smiled and said that perhaps because I lead an active life, this was precisely how God was choosing to be with me.

Since then, "resting in God" has become one of the primary ways that I pray. It's similar to an elderly married couple feeling comfortable being in each other's presence in silence. Words aren't always necessary. Nor is it important to have "fireworks" in a relationship all the time.

Certainly I enjoy times in prayer when I find a new insight, experience an emotional response to Jesus' sayings, or can imagine myself in a scene from the Gospels. But I also like simply *being* with God. Lately I've realized it can be every bit as enjoyable as the times when something seems to be "happening" in prayer.

Of course any time spent in God's presence is transformative, because God is always nourishing our hearts, soothing past hurts, and strengthening us for whatever awaits us.

In Mark's Gospel Jesus invites his disciples to "come away" so they can "rest a while" (6:31). And while that implies physical rest from all the disciples' hectic activity, it also implies a peaceful rest with Jesus himself.

So why not hear Jesus' invitation addressed to you, today, wherever you are. Can you come away from your busy life and "rest a while" in his presence?

He's waiting to meet you there.

Centering Prayer

The contemporary practice known as "centering prayer," which invites a person to encounter God in one's soul, often gets a bad rap in Catholic circles. Some people think of it as suspiciously "Zen" or "Buddhist." (As if we couldn't learn something about meditation from another tradition!)

But it's hard for me to understand these concerns, especially since St. Paul writes, "Do you not know that your body is a temple of the Holy Spirit within you, whom you have from God?" (1 Cor 6:19). Or since St. Augustine says that God is *intimior intimo meo*: nearer to me than I am to myself.

The technique of centering prayer is simple. First, you take a minute to quiet yourself down and try to rest in God's presence. Second, you choose a "prayer word" ("God," "Jesus," "love" are popular ones) and simply repeat that word in your mind. Third, if you grow distracted, you return to the prayer word and let it anchor you in God's presence.

During the prayer you may feel nothing is "happening," but sometimes you may truly feel the calming presence of God. It's essentially a prayer of "being" rather than "doing."

Centering prayer is like taking a silent walk with a good friend on a beach. You don't need to say anything; you can simply enjoy the other person's company. And even though you may not be speaking, a deeper level of conversation may be going on.

The Colloquy

To think of speaking with God as a friend may seem shocking. After all, God is the Creator of the universe. How could anyone approach God as a *friend*? But the idea of a friendship with God has a distinguished history in Catholic spirituality. St. Ignatius Loyola, the sixteenth-century founder of the Jesuit Order, encouraged this practice in his *Spiritual Exercises*.

At the close of many meditations, Ignatius suggests that we imagine ourselves speaking to Jesus "in the way one friend speaks to another . . . telling one's concerns and asking counsel." This form of prayer he calls a "colloquy," or "conversation." But note the stance Ignatius recommends: one friend to another.

Many believers engage in colloquies in a simple way: they picture Jesus in front of them, say, sitting in a chair. Then they pour out what they want to say in prayer. Your colloquy doesn't have to be only petitions. It could include thanksgiving. Or you can just let Jesus know what's going on in your life. Of course he knows *already*, but there is something consoling about sharing yourself with Jesus in this way.

Sometimes people feel comfortable enough imagining that Jesus responds. One way to do this is to imagine what Jesus *would* say. Do you have a friend you know so well that you can anticipate her responses to your problems? This way of anticipating or "intuiting" answers is another way of conversing with Jesus.

However you pray the colloquy, be open to the new ways of deepening your friendship with God.

Praying with Your Guardian Angel

Pope Francis said, "According to Church tradition, we all have an angel with us, who guards us." Earlier that day, in his private chapel, he said that we often have the feeling that "I should do this; this is not right; be careful." This, he suggested, is the voice of our guardian angel.

A skeptical Catholic may raise an eyebrow at that. But the pope is correct: the belief is part of our tradition. In the Old Testament, a variety of angels demonstrate their care for men and women. "My angel shall go before you," says God to Moses (Exod 32:34). Speaking of his "little ones," Jesus says, "their angels in heaven always see the face of my Father" (Matt 18:10). In the Acts of the Apostles, an angel rescues Peter from prison (12:6-11). Later scholars and saints, including St. Jerome, St. Thomas Aquinas, and St. John Paul II, also wrote about these angelic protectors.

The word "angel" comes from the Greek *angelos*, which means messenger. Guardian angels, then, are simply emissaries from the God who wants to protect us. Pope Francis suggested some questions we might ask about our guardian angel: "Do I listen to him? Do I bid him good day in the morning? Do I tell him: 'Guard me while I sleep'? Do I speak with him? Do I ask his advice?" (Of course we can say "her" as well.)

All of us need help. So why not ask help from the angel whom the Lord has appointed to, in the pope's words, "guard me and accompany me on the path, and who always beholds the face of the Father who is in heaven."

The Mass as Prayer

A few years ago a young Jesuit said to me, "The most surprising thing happened the other day. Right in the middle of Mass, I felt so close to God, and was moved to tears."

He then paused and laughed at what he had said.

Too often we forget that private prayer is not the only time that God communicates with us. Called by the Second Vatican Council the "source" and "summit" of Christian life, the Mass itself is a prayer, a time when God can touch us deeply.

Christ is present in four ways in the Mass: the Eucharist most of all, but also in the presider, the Scriptures, and the assembly. So as we receive the Body of Christ, listen to the readings and Gospel proclaimed (as well as the homily), pray with the priest, and participate with the congregation, we can feel a profound connection with God.

One specific way to pray at Mass is to listen attentively to the beautiful words prayed by the presider. One of my favorite lines comes in Eucharistic Prayer III: "You never cease to gather a people to yourself." The image of God's gathering us together is a consoling one for those who wonder if God cares for them. And it is not simply the individual who is drawn to God but the entire congregation in church—and people beyond.

So the next time you're at Mass, try listening carefully to the presider's words, and see if something resonates with you. What might God want to say to you?

Praying to Become What We Receive

Behold what you are; become what you receive," wrote St. Augustine in the fourth century.

When I first encountered this quote during graduate school, it set my head spinning—and changed the way I understood the Eucharist.

Augustine's famous comment reminds us that we can look at the "Body of Christ" in a number of ways, all of which overlap.

There is, first, the body of Jesus Christ, who lived on earth, suffered, died, and was raised from the dead. There is the Church as one body with many parts, an image used by St. Paul (1 Cor 12:12). There is the "Mystical Body of Christ," the Church in heaven and on earth (the subject of an encyclical by Pope Pius XII). There is the Body of Christ that is the present-day Church, the people of God throughout the world. Each reality is present in the Eucharist, which is also the Body of Christ.

Trying to unpack Augustine's profound counsel would be like trying to explain a poem. But for me, his words remind us to live in both the present and future. The knowledge that we are already part of Christ's Body is immensely comforting. But there is a future promise too: the more we partake of the Eucharist, the more Christlike we will become.

Perhaps you might use Augustine's words as an invitation to prayer—to meditate more deeply on the reality you are receiving in the Eucharist. On the reality you already are, and are called to be. That's a prayer for a lifetime.

Eucharistic Adoration

The Second Vatican Council teaches that Jesus Christ is present in four main ways during the celebration of the Mass. He is present in the words of Scripture, in the person of the presider, and in the gathering of the faithful. But Jesus is "most fully" (*maxime* is the Latin used) in the Eucharist: the bread and wine that become Jesus' Body and Blood. This is what lies behind the Catholic devotion known as "Eucharistic Adoration," during which a person prays before the consecrated bread, which is either kept in a tabernacle or "exposed" in a monstrance. A monstrance is a vessel, usually made of precious metals, used to display a host. (Monstrance means "to show.")

While many churches offer Benediction of the Blessed Sacrament, a short public prayer service, many people also enjoy praying before the Blessed Sacrament by themselves, during any time of the day. Some parishes designate special times for Eucharistic Adoration. But simply ducking into an open church for a "visit" is also a beloved tradition.

How does one pray before the Blessed Sacrament? That differs from person to person. For me, adoration helps to focus my meditations more than when I pray, for example, in my room. The prayer (or prayers) may be the same, but the visible sign—the window into the divine—is a reminder that prayer is not a monologue: there is One who listens. It is also a reminder that Christ chose simple things to make himself known to us: bread and wine. And that God also used a simple thing—a human body—to reveal himself to us "most fully."

Praying with Icons

t wasn't until I was a Jesuit novice—at age twenty-seven—that I spent any time thinking about icons, the stylized portraits of holy men and women that are part of the spiritual traditions of Eastern Christianity.

In our novitiate chapel was a lovely icon of Jesus that was painted (or "written," to use the correct term) at a nearby Orthodox monastery. For two years "Christ the Lifegiver," with a gentle-eyed Jesus holding a Bible in his left hand and offering a blessing with his right, kept me company while I prayed. His serene gaze always helped to calm me down. Without knowing it, I had started to pray with icons.

In its truest form, iconography conforms to several ancient practices. Certain symbols and colors are used to convey the particulars about the man or woman portrayed; and the icon's creation flows from the iconographer's life of prayer (and sometimes fasting).

One of the most common definitions of icons is that they are "windows into heaven." As one iconographer told me, their underlying purpose is to bring you into the presence of Jesus, Mary, or the saints and to allow you to gaze upon them as they gaze upon you. Of course you are not praying to the icons themselves; you are allowing the images, and the prayers of the person depicted in the image, to draw you into a more contemplative state. And in that state you can draw closer to God—the source of inspiration for the iconographer, for the saint portrayed, and ultimately, for you.

Images of God

What's your favorite image of God? Creator? Source of All Being? Father? Mother?

Our images of God naturally influence our relationship with God in prayer. For example, if you think of God as angry or vengeful, it may be difficult to be open and honest in prayer or to feel intimacy with God. In my experience, people sometimes relate to God in the ways they have related to other authority figures in their lives. If your parents or teachers were demanding, you may be inclined to see God as demanding.

But this can severely limit our understanding of God because, needless to say, God is not our mother or father. God is always bigger than our experiences, and our imaginations too.

One all-too-common image is God as the unforgiving judge, ready to pounce on you for the slightest transgression. Yet in the Parable of the Prodigal Son, Jesus presents us with a completely different image (Luke 15:11-32). The father welcomes home his wayward son not with condemnation and vengeance but with love and mercy. And for those who have a difficult time imagining God, I always suggest the same thing: Look at Jesus in the Gospels. Look at Jesus and you will see God.

Over time, our images of God may change, which is all to the good. As the Jesuit Carlos Valles wrote, "If you always imagine God in the same way, no matter how true and beautiful it may be, you will not be able to receive the gift of the new ways God has ready for you."

**For All
Reasons**

The Best Time to Pray

Most of us would like to find more time to pray. But that raises a question I often hear: What's the best time of day to pray? The answer, of course, is whatever time works best for you. But that still begs a few questions . . .

Let's consider a few "time-management problems" in the spiritual life and possible solutions.

The most common problem is not having enough time. If you're a young parent or a harried worker, it might feel like you have no time at all! In this case, remember two things: First, it's important to at least *try* to carve out time with God; second, *any* time in prayer is worthwhile. Try taking just five minutes for one-on-one time with God. The busier you are, the more you need it.

A second common complaint: praying at night leads you to fall asleep. This often happens when people pray the examination of conscience, the end-of-the-day review. One solution: shift that prayer to the following morning, and reflect on the prior day.

Third, people who have ever-changing schedules (students, for example) find it hard to settle on a regular prayer time. Solution: remind yourself that regularity is not the be-all and end-all of the spiritual life. Be satisfied with being with God at different times.

For me, morning is the best time to pray—before the craziness of my day begins. But you might not be a morning person. That's fine, too. God's up day and night!

Family Prayer

The family is sometimes called the *ecclesiola*, a charming Greek word meaning "little church." From the earliest days of Christianity, the family has been seen as an important place where a person's faith can be nourished. This is not the case for everyone, of course, but a great many Catholics first learn to pray in a family setting—offering grace at mealtimes, going to Mass together, and being taught nighttime prayers.

One of my favorite examples of family prayer comes from a friend who is married and has three children—two boys and one girl, now ages five through sixteen. Every night, usually at the dinner table, the family does a modified "examination of conscience," patterned on the popular Jesuit spiritual practice. Each family member is invited to recall one thing from the day for which he or she is grateful and explain it to the rest of those at the table. Often this results in some lively, and funny, stories. It also begins family dinners on an upbeat note—something else to be grateful for. Then everyone offers a brief summary of their day. After everyone has finished, together they ask God for help for the next day.

My friend tells me he's often amazed by what his children are grateful for. It helps him understand his children, and God, better.

You don't need to have children to do family prayer. You can find creative ways to pray with your parents or grandparents, uncles or aunts, cousins or stepbrothers and stepsisters. Every family prays differently, so trust that the way that your "little church" likes to pray is pleasing to God.

Praying with Friends

Catholics pray with friends every time they attend Mass. But sometimes that's it. Unlike members of other Christian denominations, for whom praying in common is, well, common, Catholics often shrink from the idea of sitting beside a friend in silent prayer or—more daunting still—praying aloud with a friend.

But I love praying with friends. Even if it's as simple as saying grace before meals, it's fascinating to hear how others speak to God. It's a privileged window into how they relate to God, and so it can strengthen your own faith. A few years ago at a restaurant, I asked a friend if she would like to say grace. She smiled, and then listed all the things about our friendship that she was grateful for. And that made *me* grateful.

Perhaps the most natural time to pray with a friend is during difficult times. After a friend shares her problems—in her family, on the job, relating to health—why not ask if you can pray aloud with her? Then you can voice her concerns to God aloud. It helps when someone else verbalizes your worries: it's a reminder that if a friend can hear you, so can God.

It's odd that many Catholics aren't all that comfortable praying in this way—at least in my experience. Maybe we're more comfortable talking *about* God together than talking *to* God together. In that case, the next time you're with a friend, and you feel moved, why not bring God into the conversation?

God's there already, but prayer is an excellent reminder of that.

Faith Sharing

One of the most enjoyable parts of my Jesuit life is "faith sharing," regular conversations with my brother Jesuits about where God has been active in our prayer and daily lives. But you don't have to be a Jesuit to participate in group faith sharing. Nor is faith sharing reserved for only priests or members of religious orders.

In my experience, here is a structure that works well: Once a month, gather together a small group of people (four to five seems optimal), and begin with a short prayer. Let everyone share, for roughly ten minutes, where they feel they have experienced God over the last few weeks. They should be encouraged to talk about their daily lives as well as their prayer. Let each person do so with no interruptions. After a few sessions, when participants have grown more comfortable with one another, people might want to respond—very, very briefly—after a person has shared, being careful never to judge, critique, or give "advice." The goal is to allow each person to share openly without fear of critique.

One of the greatest graces of faith sharing comes with seeing God's activity in other people. And often it's easier to see God's work in others than in yourself. Likewise, others can often point out God's activity in *your* life when you aren't able to notice it.

All of this is a terrific encouragement in the spiritual life. For it reminds you that even if you don't feel God's presence, God is always at work in you.

Spiritual Conversations

One of my favorite stories from the lives of the saints concerns a spiritual conversation between two siblings: St. Benedict and St. Scholastica. Both Benedict and Scholastica lived in monasteries in the sixth century and saw each other only once a year. During one visit, Scholastica asked her brother to postpone his departure so that they could continue their engrossing conversation about the spiritual life. Benedict said he needed to return to his monastery. In response, Scholastica said a brief prayer. Suddenly a thunderstorm blew in, forcing Benedict to stay.

That story, perhaps legendary, points out the value of "spiritual conversations," that is, discussing the spiritual life with a close friend, a fellow believer—or even your sibling the saint. It's different than "spiritual direction," where someone helps "guide" another person in the spiritual life. Here the conversation is between peers, with no one "directing" other than the Holy Spirit.

Listening to a friend talk about his or her experience of God can kindle your own desire to lead a holier life. The other person may have insights about prayer, for example, that you've never considered before. He or she can also nudge you to lead a holier life. For myself, I simply delight in seeing the ways that God can work within another person.

Scholastica valued her conversations with her brother. In fact, when he refused to stay, she conversed with someone else. "I asked you, and you would not listen to me," she told Benedict after the storm blew in. "So I asked my Lord, and he has listened to me."

Journaling

Many people keep a journal to record the fruits of their prayer. This is a surprisingly useful spiritual practice, since as time passes we naturally tend to forget what God has revealed to us. After all, even the disciples were prone to forgetting what Jesus had done—often right in front of them.

This forgetting may stem from plain old laziness, or more likely from a fear of responding to what we've learned in our spiritual lives. (If we remember what God has revealed to us, we might have to change!) Keeping a written record reminds us of God's activity in our lives; and by looking backward we can gain confidence in the future.

Writing a journal also has a distinguished history in the lives of the saints, from St. Augustine to Pope St. John XXIII to Servant of God Dorothy Day. Day once wrote (in her journal) that a journal helps us see how various problems "evaporate" over time.

Today this form of writing is often referred to as "journaling." This means that the writing *itself* is a form of prayer. It includes such practices as writing a letter to God, imagining a conversation between you and God, listing those things for which you are grateful, or starting with a question like "What do you want me to do for you?" and then writing an answer in God's voice.

So the next time you find yourself stuck in prayer, pick up a paper and pen. Or fire up your computer and start typing.

Everyday Mysticism

Mysticism is sometimes seen as a privileged experience for only the most well-trained of spiritual athletes. But in her book *Guidelines for Mystical Prayer*, Ruth Burrows, a Carmelite nun, says that this form of prayer is not simply the province of the saints: "For what is the mystical life but God coming to do what we cannot do; God touching the depths of our being where man is reduced to his basic element?" Karl Rahner, the twentieth-century priest and theologian, spoke of "everyday mysticism." But how can we define it?

A mystical experience is one in which you feel filled with God's presence in an intense and unmistakable way. Or you feel "lifted up" from the normal way of seeing things. Or you are overwhelmed with the sense of God in a way that transcends your understanding. Needless to say, such experiences are difficult to put into words. It's the same as trying to describe the first time you fell in love, or held your newborn child, or saw the ocean.

Sometimes people feel moved to tears, unable to contain their love or gratitude. One man described feeling almost as if he were a crystal vase, and God's love was like water about to overflow the top of the vase.

While mystical experiences are gifts, they are not as rare as some might believe. And because they are so personal, they are often hard to describe. (The saints even had a tough time with that.) But that does not mean they are not real or that they should not be reverenced—and treasured.

Spiritual Direction

If you spend enough time reading spirituality books, you'll eventually run across the term "spiritual direction." Even devout Catholics might wonder: what's that?

Spiritual directors help people with their personal relationships with God. The practice may overlap with several disciplines, but it is distinct from each. It is not psychotherapy (which often does not address spiritual experiences). It is not the sacrament of reconciliation (which focuses on sin and forgiveness). It is not pastoral counseling (which deals with a particular problem).

Spiritual direction is focused on God. With a spiritual director you discuss your experiences of prayer and of God in daily life. In a tradition that goes back to the desert fathers and mothers, spiritual directors do not make decisions for you; rather, they invite you to see where God is active in your life, encourage you to notice where you are overlooking God's gentle voice, and help you to reflect on your prayer. The best directors do so with total freedom, allowing God to do God's own work. Also, directors are not simply holy men and women; they are trained in techniques for listening and for seeing how God is at work. Many spend years in professional programs before beginning to direct.

How can you find a spiritual director? Try contacting a retreat house or checking a web site like Spiritual Directors International. After a few sessions with a spiritual director you'll see how fruitful it is to have someone help you grow in awareness of God's gracious activity. But the real director, as any good spiritual director will tell you, is the Holy Spirit.

Christian Retreats

While many corporations ask their employees to go on retreats these days, the practice began not in the corporate world but the spiritual one. Essentially, a retreat is an extended period of time spent with God in prayer, usually in silence.

Christian retreats originated in Jesus' practice of "withdrawing" from his disciples to pray in what the Gospels call "a secluded place." Jesus needed time away from the crowds, and he craved one-on-one time with God the Father.

Retreats take place in a variety of settings. Often people go to a retreat house, sometimes a big, rambling building located far from the din of daily activity. There are different forms of a retreat. On a *directed retreat* a person sees a spiritual director on a daily basis to discuss what is happening in prayer. A *guided retreat* focuses on a particular topic (say, women's spirituality) and offers presentations and the opportunity to meet with a director, though less frequently than during a directed retreat. *Preached retreats* consist in listening to presentations and praying on your own but with fewer opportunities for direction.

Many retreats are done in silence, which helps retreatants better notice the subtle movements of God in their prayer. For me, my annual eight-day retreat is a high point of the year; it's often when I feel closest to God.

For more information, why not ask your local parish or diocese about nearby retreat houses, to see where you might deepen your one-on-one relationship with God.

Beginning with Gratitude

Finding your prayer dry? Having a tough time seeing God in your daily life? Struggling with despair? Then begin with gratitude, the easiest way to jump-start your spiritual life.

One of the most popular ways to pray is St. Ignatius Loyola's "examination of conscience," in which you review the day to discover signs of God's activity. And, surprisingly for a man of his times, Ignatius begins the prayer not with a catalogue of one's sins but with gratitude.

Why? Well, left to our own devices, we tend to focus on the negatives in life. Many of us are also inveterate problem solvers. Thus, when we look back on our day we automatically focus on what went wrong, on what needs to be fixed. Some of this is part of our emotional hardwiring, the vestige of the prehistoric mind: the caveman or cavewoman most likely to survive was the one most alert to danger. But concentrating on our problems can mean we overlook our blessings.

What if you don't feel that you have much to be grateful for? In that case, try looking at smaller, everyday blessings. The taste of a peanut butter and jelly sandwich. A crazy joke that lightened your day. An unexpected phone call from a friend. Or look at more long-term blessings: a roof over your head, food on the table, a job. To be grateful, all you need to do is recall the blessing, savor it, and tell God that you're thankful.

As Meister Eckhart wrote, "If the only prayer you ever say in your entire life is 'Thank you,' that will be enough."

Honesty in Prayer

What happens if you tell a friend, a spouse, or a relative only what you think they want to hear? Or if you talk only about topics you think won't upset them? Or if you share only the parts of your life that don't embarrass you? Usually what happens is this: over time your formerly warm relationship grows cool. Soon it becomes overly formal, even distant.

Something similar can happen in the spiritual life. Many people feel embarrassed about sharing certain things with God in prayer: anger or frustration, for example. Even though God has dealt with such emotions for as long as the psalms ("How long, O Lord?" begins Psalm 13), people resist sharing raw emotions with God.

Likewise, many people resist asking for help when they need it because it seems "selfish." In both these cases—anger and need—people are sometimes not honest in prayer. In time, they start to feel distanced from God. You've probably heard the saying: "If you feel that God is distant, guess who moved?"

Even though God knows how we are feeling, it helps to share our innermost thoughts and feelings, not simply because it helps to get things "off our chest," but because God desires an intimate relationship with us.

So when it comes to prayer, be honest. Honesty, even about painful emotions or urgent needs, will help you feel closer to the God who wants to console, comfort—and, most of all, listen.

I'm Angry, God!

Jesus is fully human and fully divine. And, among other things, "fully human" means that Jesus is like us in all things, except sin. That means he experienced the full range of human emotions: joy, sadness—and anger. The Gospels are clear on this: Jesus got angry. "O faithless and perverse generation . . . how long will I endure you?" he says to the disciples (Matt 17:17). He curses a fig tree for not bearing fruit (Mark 11:12-14). He upends the merchants' tables in the temple (Matt 21:12). Jesus' anger, however, was always on behalf of others.

Anger is a natural and inevitable part of life. This is not to say you should be furious all the time—if this is the case, you need to examine things. But how can you pray when you are angry? First, it's helpful to think about *why* you're angry. Is it your wounded pride? Or has someone critiqued you for a good reason? Just because people are criticizing you doesn't mean that you're being "persecuted"—you might just be wrong. Perhaps you're called to greater humility. Or are you incensed because of a tiny inconvenience? In that case, maybe you need some perspective.

But perhaps you're angry for a deeper reason. Someone has died. You are very ill. You've lost your job. In that case, it's time to speak with God honestly about your feelings. God can handle it. God has been listening to anger and frustration in prayer since at least the time of the psalms: "How long, O Lord?" begins Psalm 13.

So be angry, but also be honest about where the anger comes from—and then open your heart to God.

Prayers of Petition

Many people tell me they feel guilty asking for things in prayer. They fear it's selfish. "Why should I ask for things when so many people have it worse than me?" they say. Or, "Am I not supposed to accept God's will?"

It's true that many people are worse off than we are; and ultimately we are indeed invited to accept God's plans. But before that comes honesty. God wants us to be honest in prayer, because God wants us to be ourselves. That means asking for help when we need it. For if we say only what we think we "should" say in prayer, our relationship with God is bound to grow cold. Part of being honest is admitting when we need help.

Besides, Jesus invites us to ask God for help, giving us the parable of the persistent widow who keeps asking and asking (Luke 18). "Ask, and you shall receive," after all, presupposes asking. Jesus also counsels us to ask for "our daily bread," which is another form of petitionary prayer. And notice that in the Garden of Gethsemane, in Jesus' own hour of need, he said to the Father, "Remove this cup from me" (Luke 22:42). Jesus did not wish to die. But when he realized it was the divine plan, he accepted it. But it all started with his honest prayer to the Father.

We don't always get exactly what we ask for in prayer: that's obvious. But as human beings we must ask, because God desires our honesty. In a sense, such an intimate relationship with God is the answer to our prayers.

Insights in Prayer

There is an unfortunate tendency in some Christian spiritual circles to privilege the emotional over the intellectual. Spiritual directors (myself included) often emphasize how God can work through your emotional life—moving you to tears during a Mass, prompting feelings of consolation when reading Scripture, or filling you with joy at the sight of a sunrise. Sometimes this emphasis, however, can lead to downplaying intellectual insights that happen in prayer. But God is just as likely to work through our minds as through our hearts.

One example is having an "Aha" moment while praying with Scripture. A few years ago, I was reading the story of Jesus' rejection in his hometown synagogue in Nazareth (Luke 4:16-30). Almost all the homilies I had heard about this passage focused on how the townspeople knew Jesus too well and thus dismissed him. How could someone living among them be the Messiah?

But during my prayer, I realized something I had never thought about: Jesus knew *them* too. When we know people well, we can usually predict how they might respond to something controversial we might say. Jesus surely knew that his comments could provoke controversy. But he preached the Good News anyway. For me, it was an important realization about the courage required for Christian discipleship. This was an intellectual insight and not one that came with a great deal of emotion. God was just as much at work through my intellect as if God had moved me to tears.

So when it comes to prayer: trust your heart . . . but use your head, too.

Pilgrimage as Prayer

Did you ever think of Jesus as making a pilgrimage? It may seem odd to imagine the Son of God in that light, but remember that when he was twelve, Jesus accompanied Mary and Joseph on a pilgrimage to Jerusalem (Luke 2:41). (That's when his parents lost track of him and discovered him in the Temple.) Later, the Gospel of John records Jesus journeying several times to Jerusalem for the Jewish feasts. In fact, Jesus was crucified, died, and rose again during a time of pilgrimage—Passover. So Christian pilgrimage, which finds its roots in Jewish pilgrimage, is as old as Jesus.

A pilgrimage is a journey undertaken for a spiritual purpose. Often it is to a holy site like Jerusalem, Rome, or Lourdes. The final destination may move us: seeing the sites where Jesus walked, the martyrs were killed, or Mary appeared can evoke powerful emotions within us. But the journey itself is often illuminating: tired, removed from our daily routines, and surrounded by new friends, we are invited to move beyond familiar boundaries and encounter God in new ways. Prayer on pilgrimage is usually different from prayer in our rooms—which is a good thing.

But all of life is a pilgrimage. We journey alongside others, notice God along the way, and are graced with surprises, until we finally meet the One whom we long to see. God is with us in all our life's travels and meets us at the end of the journey.

As St. Catherine of Siena said, "All the way to heaven is heaven, because he said, 'I am the Way.'"

Nature Prayer

During a retreat a few years ago, a woman came to me for spiritual direction. "What was your prayer like yesterday?" I asked. "Wonderful!" she said. "I hugged a tree!" I had to suppress a laugh. Was she kidding?

She was not. "When I stretched my arms around that big tree outside, I felt connected to a living creation of God, I felt rooted to the earth, and I felt a sense of God's presence in nature." Now I was smiling for a different reason: her words touched my heart.

This woman had encountered God through creation, what we refer to as "Nature Prayer." Here are a few ways to do it. *First*, be aware of the natural world God created. Have you noticed the leaves on the trees lately? The ever-changing patterns of the clouds? When was the last time you saw—I mean really saw—a sunset? Nature can move us to be grateful for beauty in our lives. *Second*, ponder how, as St. Ignatius Loyola said, God "labors" in creation. God sustains the plants and animals— and us—by breathing life into them and keeping them alive. What a wonder! *Finally*, try using nature to "image" God. For example, whenever I'm at the seashore, I think of the waves as images of God's care. As each wave breaks upon the beach and recedes, I imagine God carrying away my worries. Obviously the waves themselves are not God, but they help me in my prayer.

I'm glad I didn't laugh when the retreatant told me she hugged a tree. Because, in the end, she changed the way I find God in nature.

Praying for Our Common Home

My favorite part of Pope Francis's encyclical on the environment, *Laudato Si': On the Care of Our Common Home*, is a brief section called "The Gaze of Jesus." It changed the way I look at creation.

Most of us already know, in a deep way, that God lived among creation in the person of Jesus. We also know that Jesus often used images from nature—seeds, birds, clouds, wheat, fish—in his parables to help people understand the reign of God. But Pope Francis offers us a fresh insight in *Laudato Si'*, which is that Jesus *enjoyed* creation:

"The Lord was able to invite others to be attentive to the beauty that there is in the world because he himself was in constant touch with nature, lending it an attention full of fondness and wonder. As he made his way throughout the land, he often stopped to contemplate the beauty sown by his Father, and invited his disciples to perceive a divine message in things" (97).

What a wonderful invitation to pray with creation! The next time you find yourself in the midst of nature, can you "stop to contemplate the beauty sown" by God? Allow nature—whether you are standing at the ocean, in a forest, or before a sunset—to lead you to an appreciation of God as the creator of all things.

That appreciation will naturally lead you to pray for creation, "our common home." And then to work and advocate for this beautiful world, into which God has placed you.

Summertime Prayer

Ahhh summer! Of course it can have its problems. In the northeastern United States, where I live, those problems include occasional droughts, humidity that tempts you to spend entire days standing in front of an air conditioner, and far too many mosquitoes. By the way, when I get to heaven I plan to ask God why he made those particular insects: Couldn't God have given the birds something to eat that didn't also suck our blood?

But, overall, I love summer and also find it an easy time to pray. For one thing, the season makes it easy to appreciate the glory of God's creation. So one suggestion for summertime prayer is to contemplate your favorite growing thing and let it "speak" to you about how God works. Is there a glorious maple tree in your front yard that you've seen grow slowly over the last few years? Think of how God helps *you* to grow—slowly but surely. Does your garden astonish you with its variety of flowers? Remember that we're all plants in God's garden, and all of us make that garden look beautiful.

And let the summer remind you of God's promise to make all things new. Just a few months ago in the Northeast, in the cold depths of winter, everything seemed irredeemably dead. It seemed hard to believe that anything new could come out of that cold earth. But look around now—so much life! Remember that nothing is impossible with God, and that God can always bring new life out of seemingly dead situations.

Growth, variety, new life . . . surely those things are worth a few mosquito bites!

Finding God in All Things

If you asked five Jesuits from five different countries to sum up Ignatian spirituality, which is based on the life and teachings of their founder, St. Ignatius Loyola, they would probably say the same thing: "Finding God in all things." Oddly enough, that phrase isn't found in Ignatius's writings; rather, it's something one of the early Jesuits recounted the saint saying.

What does it mean? Simply put, God is to be found not only in obvious places—like church services, private prayer, and reading the Bible—but everywhere and in everything: in our busy workplaces, in our quirky families, and even when we are by ourselves, feeling lonely. Every moment is an invitation to experience God.

This doesn't mean that every second of our day will feel like a life-changing epiphany, but it does mean that Jesus' invitation to "Come and see" applies not just to the disciples in first-century Palestine but to us, today. God is saying, "Come, look at your day, and see where I am."

How can we do this? By noticing. When you speak with someone, can you see your conversation as a holy moment of encounter? Perhaps they're struggling—God may be inviting you to care for them. When you eat a meal, can you be grateful for the nourishment and also remember that it's God who is feeding you? When a sunbeam hits the carpet, can you rejoice in the beauty of creation? At the end of the day, it helps to remember these things—all things—and be grateful you've found God. And, more important, that God has found you.

Savoring

Many of us lead busy lives and are constantly rushing around. As a result, it's hard to slow down and, as the saying goes, "smell the roses."

That can be a problem because it means we often don't pause to take stock of life's blessings. Moreover, we seem to be hardwired to pay closer attention to problems rather than to blessings. Psychologists suggest this may be a remnant from our prehistoric past, when human beings needed to be hypervigilant about danger. The caveman or cavewoman who was attentive to physical threats was more likely to survive than the contemplative person, who would be more likely to be eaten up by a fearsome beast while he or she was dreamily pondering a sunset!

Those two tendencies—to rush and to focus on the negative—can be combated with savoring. In his *Spiritual Exercises*, St. Ignatius Loyola recommends that the one praying "relish" or "savor" certain spiritual moments. For Ignatius this meant returning to a particular prayer that held great fruit. It can also mean recalling something that happened during your day, or in your life, for which you are grateful and revisiting it in prayer. You do this almost as if savoring a good meal, reveling in it—slowly and deliberately enjoying it. Then you express thanks to God. Such gratitude is a foundation of the spiritual life because it helps us to see how much we depend on God, and how much God freely gives us.

As the thirteenth-century German mystic Meister Eckhart said, "If the only prayer you ever say in your entire life is 'Thank you,' it will be enough."

Joy and Prayer

I have said these things to you so that my joy may be in you and your joy may be complete." That's Jesus in the Gospel of John (15:11). Do we believe him?

Joy runs like a bright thread through the Old and New Testaments. Abraham and Sarah laugh for joy at the improbable birth of their son Isaac. The very first word of the very first psalm is "happy." Jesus speaks of joy, the disciples experience joy at the resurrection, and St. Paul lists joy as one of the fruits of the Holy Spirit.

So why do we have a hard time including joy in our prayer?

Perhaps because we sometimes forget that Jesus of Nazareth was joyful, delighting in the company of children, enjoying himself at wedding parties, and visiting friends like Mary, Martha, and Lazarus. He is not just the "Man of Sorrows" but the "Man of Joys."

So the next time you pray, why not make a list of the things that bring you joy? That list could include something funny that your children or grandchildren, or nieces or nephews, said to you. Or things that consistently cause joy, like the good humor of a close friend. Or the deep-down knowledge that Christ is risen and that he has promised to be with you always. Make a "joy inventory," and then share that with God in prayer. Think of God listening to you and being joyful with you in turn.

Smile with God, and imagine God smiling with you. And let your joy be complete.

Being a Contemplative in Action

Jesuits often say that the goal of Ignatian spirituality—the spiritual practices based on the life and writings of St. Ignatius Loyola—is to become a "contemplative in action." But it's just as accurate to see this as a goal of the Christian life in general.

For many people, the goal of living a life with a contemplative heart may seem elusive. So besides intentionally carving out time for private prayer, how can we become contemplatives in action?

One way to live contemplatively is to see each person, each place, and each moment as an invitation to encounter God. In the abstract, this sounds easy. Every friendly face, every sunny day, and every happy occasion makes seeing God easy.

But how about the more difficult people, places, and moments? Can you see these occasions as inviting you into a closer relationship with God? Is the difficult person in your office an invitation to deeper charity? Is being caught in the rain without your umbrella an invitation to be less concerned over your favorite coat getting wet? Is the traffic jam an invitation to patience?

Overall, are these difficult moments inviting you to greater freedom and therefore a greater ability to be closer to God?

It is easy to recognize the difficult situations and people that come our way. The question a contemplative heart asks is: are we open to letting them change us, free us, and move us closer to God?

Praying as Priest, Prophet, and King

You probably have seen the phrase "by virtue of your baptism." This means that baptism confers on us certain graces and privileges, one of which is participation in the "threefold office" of Jesus—priest, prophet, and king.

Jesus served as "priest" since he offered himself as a sacrifice to the Father and serves as a mediator between us and the Father. Clearly he was a "prophet" in all he said and did on earth. And he is a "king" who said he came not to be served but to serve—a servant leader.

How might this threefold ministry influence us?

First, if we are praying, we are carrying out a "priestly" ministry. The daily sacrifices we make for others are prayers in action. Like Jesus the High Priest, we also offer our lives to God and invite others into a relationship with God. *Second*, while we are not called to preach the Sermon on the Mount as Jesus the Prophet did, we are all called to lead prophetic lives. We might do this by speaking out for the voiceless or by challenging unethical practices in the workplace. *Finally*, while few (none) of us are members of a royal family, we are called to exercise leadership both in the Church and in the world. We do so not by lording our authority over others but by serving them and helping them grow—empowering them to become leaders in their own way.

So one suggestion for prayer is to ask: *Where have I exercised these roles in the past? Where am I now exercising them? And where can I exercise them in new places?*

Because you are indeed called to be priest, prophet, and king. By virtue of your baptism.

God Speaks through Dreams

Does God speak to us through dreams? There are two ways to answer that question: yes and yes.

First, if you look at the Bible, the answer is *yes*. Dreams are an important way that God speaks to people in both the Old and New Testaments. In the book of Genesis, God speaks to Joseph in a highly symbolic dream, filled with imagery like sheaves of wheat and hungry cows, which helps Joseph see what lies ahead for him and his family.

In the New Testament, another Joseph—Mary's husband—learns that Mary is not pregnant through relations with another man but has miraculously conceived Jesus. In a subsequent dream Joseph is told to take his wife and infant son to Egypt to flee the murderous Herod.

Second, if you look at people's experiences of dreams today, the answer is also *yes*. Of course few of us (as far as I know) have dreams that foretell the future. But God sometimes uses dreams to invite us to see things that our conscious minds might be reluctant to see. Perhaps when our conscious minds resist, God works through our unconscious—which, after all, God created. In my work as a spiritual director I often invite people to pay attention to dreams that seem especially meaningful. I ask them: *What occurs to you about this dream? What might God be inviting you to see in a new way?*

You probably won't be asked to flee to Egypt, but in dreams God may be revealing something to you in a surprising way. Pay attention to your dreams—like both Josephs did.

Praying for Mercy

When Pope Francis inaugurated the Year of Mercy in December 2015, I was asked the same question by several Catholics: "Are we supposed to be merciful for only a year? What happens when the year ends?"

Needless to say, Pope Francis intended to emphasize mercy, not to limit it. In fact, you could say that his entire papacy has focused on that theme. The same might be said—with only a few quibbles from New Testament scholars—of Jesus' ministry.

There are countless ways in which you are called to be merciful (pick one): to your spouse, your family members, your coworkers, and your neighbors; not to mention the poor, the sick, the marginalized, and, as Pope Francis reminded us in his encyclical *Laudato Si'*, the earth. Creation itself deserves our mercy.

So let me suggest one person you might have forgotten to have mercy on: you. Of course you can always pray that God in his infinite compassion might look upon you mercifully. But God is already looking at you with mercy. So why not also pray that you might look upon yourself mercifully. That you might give yourself a break for all that you do. That, as one of my spiritual directors liked to say, you might be "easy with yourself."

Why not ask God to help you see yourself as God sees you: someone who is trying his or her best. Why not honor and extend the Year of Mercy by being merciful to someone God cares for very much: you.

Praying to Discern Our Vocations

What am I meant to do? Who am I meant to become? These are challenging questions for believers. For anyone. We long to know our vocations. And by vocation (from the Latin *vocare*, "to call") I don't mean simply what we're meant to do, but who we're meant to become.

An important place to begin is with desire. God calls us to the work we're meant to do through our natural attractions. A young woman might be drawn to her career as a physician through an interest in science classes in elementary school. A young man might be drawn to a career as a journalist through his enjoyment of writing for his high school newspaper. Someone interested in the priesthood or religious life might be intrigued by the life of a priest, brother, or sister who clearly enjoys serving others.

The same dynamic is at work in terms of our larger vocations: becoming who we are. Most of us have an idea of the person we would like to become one day. We may want to be more generous, or more open-minded, or less prone to complaining. Those desires are one way that God invites us to become the people we're meant to be. That's a "call" too. It's important to pray to have your deepest desires revealed—not just your surface wants but the ones that help you chart your life's course. What attracts you? What moves you?

Our deepest desires are God's desires for us. It may take a long time for us to see them clearly. But it's worth the wait. For God's plan for us is a fulfilling and holy life. God's most fundamental call is the call to happiness.

Memories in Prayer

One of the most underappreciated ways that God can speak to us is through memories. When meditating on a particular Scripture passage, for instance, a powerful memory may come to mind. Often people dismiss this as a mere distraction. But God can work through every part of our consciousness—our imaginations, our emotions, and our memories.

There are (at least) two ways of allowing God to work through memory. The first is *unintentional.* Perhaps you are going through a tough time, and life seems hopeless. Suddenly you recall an earlier period when things seemed just as bleak, but when you were also supported by friends or family. This may not be a coincidence but a way in which God is gently reminding you of God's provident care.

The second way is *intentional.* Here you explicitly choose to pray with your memories. Recently, for example, my mother sold her house. It was both a hopeful time (she was moving to a lovely new apartment) and a sad one (our family had lived in this home for fifty years). A few weeks before she moved, I invited Jesus in prayer to sit with me in each room as we recalled various events that had happened to me as a boy, an adolescent, and a young adult. Here is the desk at which I learned to write; here are the stairs I raced down on Christmas morning; here is the table on which our Thanksgiving dinners were set. It filled me with gratitude.

At the close of the prayer, when I thought perhaps Jesus would invite me to "shut the door" on those times, I realized that those events were always accessible to me—through the gift of memory.

Desires in Prayer

Desire is an essential part of a healthy spiritual life. For in our deepest desires God's desires for us are revealed. A married couple, for instance, is drawn together out of multiple desires—physical, emotional, spiritual—in order to live a life of mutual love. Desire plays a critical part in discerning any vocation: a particular job or profession, or the priesthood or religious life.

So pay attention to the holy desires that arise in prayer. You may experience a longing to follow Jesus more closely. To emulate one of the saints. Or simply to become a more loving person.

This is one reason why St. Ignatius Loyola asks us to "pray for what you want and desire" when approaching God: your holy desires reveal God's desires for you. And over time, you'll gradually learn how to discern between selfish wants (I want a new smartphone) and holy desires (I want to become a better Christian).

It's also important to pray for the simpler things you desire, as long as they are not immoral. Sometimes Catholics feel guilty about praying for healing from an illness, for example. But asking humbly for what you desire is part of being *honest* with God.

Ultimately, your deepest desire is for God. The insatiable longing for union with the divine comes from the core of your being. And that longing is planted within you by God.

For God's deep desire is union with *you*.

Distractions in Prayer

Everyone gets distracted during prayer—including the saints. St. Ignatius Loyola once wrote in his journal about being bothered by someone's whistling. Even when we feel completely centered in prayer, a stray thought can pop up: "I forgot to take out the trash!"

There are two types of distractions: unimportant and important.

Unimportant ones simply take you away from prayer. And there are many imaginative techniques to deal with them. You can think of them as clouds (or bubbles, birds, or balloons, as a friend once memorably suggested) that come into the horizon of your prayer and just float away. You notice them, but they don't trouble you.

It's important to at least *try* to let go of these distractions, as you would when talking to a friend. You want to give God your undivided attention. On the other hand, sometimes we need to admit that distractions are unavoidable. In these times, it helps to say, "I'm distracted, God, but I'm with you anyway."

Important distractions, on the other hand, may be invitations for reflection. A young Jesuit once said to me, "Every time I pray, I keep getting distracted by the memory of a person I had a fight with."

Maybe it's not a distraction, I suggested. God may be asking you to look at that in prayer.

In time, you'll get to know what to pay attention to, and what to let . . . float away.

Dryness in Prayer

When the letters of Mother Teresa were published in 2007 as *Come Be My Light*, many were stunned by what they read. After a series of mystical experiences that led her to found the Missionaries of Charity, Mother Teresa felt an absence of God in her prayer for the rest of her life. Over time, she came to see this darkness as a way of identifying with the abandoned Christ on the cross and with the poor, who often feel abandoned.

Dryness in prayer is not unusual. In fact, it is to be expected. Nearly every saint reports it. As in any relationship, there are times when it feels like not much is "happening." Sometimes when you close your eyes to pray, you might sit quietly for an hour and feel . . . nothing.

What to do? St. Ignatius Loyola suggested three things: pray more, take on some penances, and remind yourself that prayer is a gift. Also, in these times it's essential to look for God in your daily life—not inside but outside.

One of Mother Teresa's spiritual directors once told me a story, now widely known: After Mother Teresa had shared her feelings about God's absence, her spiritual director witnessed a young boy run up to Mother Teresa and throw his arms around her. Her wise director said, "Mother, that hug is God's presence, too."

In time, things change, and prayer again becomes satisfying. But even if you feel like nothing is happening, something always is—because any time spent in the presence of God is transformative. "I will be with you always," says Jesus, and he is.

Even if you can't tell.

Praying in Times of Doubt

The apostle Thomas usually gets a bad rap.

To begin with, people often forget his faithful following of Jesus. In the Gospel of John, for example, when Jesus is about to return to Judea to heal Lazarus, some of the disciples protest that it will be dangerous. By contrast, Thomas says he will stand by Jesus (John 11:16). But instead of this incident, Thomas is remembered as a "doubter" for his skepticism over initial reports of the resurrection (John 20:24-29).

Who can blame him? Sometimes it's hard to believe when things look bleak. But notice how the Risen Christ responds to Thomas's doubt. He does not castigate him, saying, "What a terrible person you are!" Instead he is compassionate, giving Thomas what he needs—physical proof of the resurrection.

It's a reminder not only that it's human to doubt but also that God is open to hearing our doubts. Even Jesus expressed a form of doubt on the cross, crying out, "My God, my God why have you forsaken me?" (Here he was doubting not God's existence but God's nearness.)

Doubt is a natural part of our lives, and if we are honest in prayer we need to share our doubt with God.

But we also need to be open to seeing where God is at work. Doubt should not blind us to the places where God is active in our lives. We can become so focused on where we think God *isn't* that we overlook where God *is*. In the end, we may even have an experience like Thomas, who, when finally given what he asked for was able to say, "My Lord and my God!"

Praying for Our Enemies

s there anything more difficult than forgiving our enemies? Yes: praying for them. Forgiveness may be slightly
easier because, at least in some cases, you find yourself
able to "move on." That is, once you find the grace to forgive people who have hurt you—and this can take weeks,
months, and even years—you often feel free to put a painful chapter of your life behind you. You can say, "I'm glad
that's over."

Praying for your enemies, by contrast, takes more spiritual work because it forces you to make those who are
hurting you *in the present*. Then you go even further, and
do something positive: pray for them. Yet this is what Jesus
asks of us (Matt 5:44).

Not long ago, I met a 93-year-old Jesuit with a great
sense of good cheer. I asked if he had any secrets to living
peacefully in a religious community. "Well," he said, "I do
get bothered sometimes by the people I live with!" But
when he struggles with someone's behavior, he first thinks
of the good that the person has done. (Admittedly, it is
hard to see anything good in people who have harmed,
persecuted, or abused you.) The Jesuit then asks to see the
person as *God* sees them. This second insight has always
been helpful for me. Most likely, these people have themselves been mistreated; insecurity may underlie their cru-
elty, and their insensitive behaviors are often indicative of
their own emotional suffering. Understanding and even
pitying people makes it easier to pray for them.

As I said, it's hard. But once done, you may feel more
free of anger or resentment. So in the end it can be a gift
both to you and to those for whom you have prayed.

**In All
Seasons**

A Season of Waiting

Waiting is a lost virtue. And technology has only contributed to this loss. No need to wait in line to buy movie tickets any longer—buy them online. No need to wait to read the latest issue of a magazine—read it online. These days we can grow impatient when our computers take more than a few seconds to load.

That's why Advent can serve as a reminder of the holiness of waiting. Faithful hope is a virtue, a grace, even a joy. Many expectant mothers have told me that while they eagerly look forward to the birth of their child, the pregnancy itself is filled with joy. "I'll miss having my baby inside of me," one mother said to me. Perhaps Mary felt the same about Jesus.

Paradoxically, Christian waiting also encourages us to find God in our present—not simply in our future. God is not only coming; God is already here. So while we anticipate the future with hope, we know that living mindfully in the present is a key way to encounter God. Remember that God does not say to Moses in Exodus, "I was" or "I will be." God says, "I am." Here and now.

One of the great joys of Christianity, however, is that God always has something good prepared for our future. For the people of Israel it was a messiah. For us now it is greater intimacy with Christ, who is alive in the Spirit. And for us at the end of our earthly lives, it is eternal life.

Find God today—but wait in hope for a beautiful future.

Patience in Prayer

One of my favorite prayers is taken from a letter written by the French Jesuit, author, and paleontologist Pierre Teilhard de Chardin, who died in 1955. It's a passage urging the young recipient to be patient.

"Above all," it begins, "trust in the slow work of God. We are quite naturally impatient in everything to reach the end without delay." The prayer suggests patience in all things, especially patience with yourself.

Advent is a season centered on patience. The central image of Advent, after all, is an expectant mother: Mary carrying Jesus. But this is not simply a dull wait, as you might wait for the traffic light to turn green at an intersection. It's a hopeful waiting, confident that God is about to do something exciting and that whatever God brings will be more than you imagine.

Still, waiting can be hard. And perhaps the most difficult thing is waiting for yourself to change. We all have an image of who we hope to become one day: perhaps kinder, freer, more generous. And we don't seem to get there. Or, rather, we don't seem to get there fast enough.

In those times I always remember an experience on a retreat. I was lamenting to my retreat director that I wasn't changing fast enough. I felt stuck.

"Look out that window," he said. It was a summer's day. "What color is that tree?" "Green," I said, referring to a large maple. "What color is it in the fall?" he said. "Red," I said. My retreat director said, "And no one sees it change."

Trust in the slow work of God.

No, Less, Yes

Can I make a confession? I'm starting to dislike Christmas.

Before you ask me to hand in my collar, let me clarify. When I say "Christmas" I mean the unpleasant cultural trappings that have almost suffocated the holiday: overheated stores packed with stressed-out shoppers; the pressure people feel to buy, buy, buy; and the endless commercials that make the season feel more about spending money than about anything else.

Is it possible to set aside the unhealthy aspects of Christmas and focus on the Nativity of Our Lord? Yes, and let me suggest three ways to do so.

First, *just say no*. You don't have to go to every party, send a card to every friend, or buy a gift for every family member. Saying no to one thing (a party) means saying yes to something else (time to pray). Second, *just say less*. Try sending three-quarters as many cards or buying half the gifts you did last year. Third, *just say yes*. Choose events that are more spiritual (church services, lessons and carols) as a way to nourish yourself and prepare for the real Christmas.

Overall, it's important to pull back from the craziness and to carve out more time for prayer during the Advent and Christmas season. Happily, the beautiful readings of Advent easily invite us to prayer.

Christ wants to enter into your life in a new way during these holy weeks. But if you're in a store listening to two people fight over a video game, you may not hear him.

Praying with the Holy Family

We think of them as nearly perfect, and perhaps they were. After all, Jesus was fully human and fully divine, Mary was conceived without sin, and Joseph was a saint. But we also need to remember that the Holy Family was a human family living in difficult times.

This means they faced many of the same struggles that families do today—worrying about money, to begin with. The Greek word the Gospels use for Joseph's profession (*tekton*) means not only carpenter but, more precisely, craftsman. That meant working with wood, of course, but also building walls, and often scrounging for work. Mary had to undergo the physical pains of childbirth and, later, mourned the death of Joseph. (He's not present at the Crucifixion, so we can presume that he had died by then.) And there were misunderstandings in this family too. When Jesus was "lost" in the temple, his parents were frantic with worry about their young son. "I was in my Father's house," Jesus assures them. "But they did not understand" (Luke 3:48-50). The next time you think your family is the only one that deals with misunderstandings, think again.

Praying with the Holy Family may mean imagining sitting in the presence of the three and remembering that their lives were not without difficulties. In this way, they are more like our own families or religious communities than we might think. But they met all their trials with love, hope, and trust. Can we?

Praying during Lent

As many Catholics approach Lent, they think: "I've got to give something up!" But here's another way of thinking about the season: as a time to explore new ways of prayer. For example, if you like to pray with the daily Gospel readings, you might instead use the prayers of the Mass (like the beautiful prefaces to the eucharistic prayers for Sundays in Lent) as something new.

My favorite way to pray is to use this season as a period of self-examination and conversion. Each Lent I ask myself: "What do I most want to change about myself? Where might God want me to grow in love?" Then, at the end of every day, I sit quietly with God for a few moments and look at this particular area. Often I imagine myself in conversation with Jesus about this aspect of my life, and I ask for his healing and grace.

But one needs to be patient when it comes to change. Conversion isn't a once-and-for-all event. It takes time, even a lifetime. Try not to grow frustrated if you're not changing "fast enough."

It's something like watching a child grow up. A few years ago, when one of my nephews was seven or eight, I told him that I was amazed at how tall he was getting.

"Uncle Jim," he said, "I look in the mirror every day and I can't see myself growing. But every time you come you tell me that!"

Trust in God's ability to help you to change, and grow, even if you don't think it's fast enough, and even if you don't see it. Because God does.

Kindness as Prayer

Every year when Ash Wednesday rolls around, Catholics usually ask one another what they're giving up for Lent. Sometimes there's also some good-natured teasing about the perceived degree of difficulty: "Is that all? That's not hard!"

This Lent, rather than giving up chocolate, why not do this: *be kind*. Kindness is an underappreciated way to lead a Christian life. Let me suggest three ways to be kind.

First, *don't be a jerk*. You may be sick, tired, or upset about some minor catastrophe that happened at work or at home. That doesn't mean that you have to pass along your anger or frustration to others. Once I said to a friend, with mock seriousness, "My life is such a cross." "Really?" he said. "For you or for others?" While it's important to share your struggles with friends, you don't need to make others miserable.

Second, *honor the absent*. Stop talking about people behind their backs. Few things are as damaging to our spiritual lives as denigrating other people. It's a serious lack of charity, and needless to say, it makes the other person feel terrible if they discover what you said—which they usually do.

Third, *give people the benefit of the doubt*. St. Ignatius Loyola mentions this at the beginning of his *Spiritual Exercises*. Whenever there is any doubt about what someone said or did, give him or her the "plus sign."

Being kind may be harder to do than giving up chocolate, but it's a lot more helpful for your spiritual life—and for everyone else's.

Fasting as Prayer

You probably know the guidelines for Lenten fasting. On Ash Wednesday and Good Friday, Catholics between the ages of 18 and 59 are to fast, that is, to eat only one full meal, without meat. On other Lenten Fridays they abstain from meat. But how does this relate to our spiritual lives?

The Gospel of Matthew describes three foundations of Jewish piety: *almsgiving*, *prayer*, and *fasting*.

The three are interconnected. For early Christians, fasting was a way of not only disciplining one's body but also saving money on food, which would then be given to the poor. St. Augustine and St. John Chrysostom both wrote that fasting without almsgiving wasn't proper. The practice also deepens our solidarity with the poor, for whom involuntary hunger is a terrible way of life. In the 1990s, when I worked with refugees in Kenya, I was often a guest in their homes and saw how little they ate. It made me think twice about wasting food in my Jesuit community.

But where does prayer come in? First, fasting deepens an awareness of our radical need for God to nourish us—both physically and spiritually. Second, when fasting reminds us of the plight of the poor, it should prompt us to *act*: to minister to the poor, advocate for them, and give alms. Third, fasting reminds us that we do not need to be ruled by every physical need. Fasting is a kind of physical prayer that calls us to remember our reliance on God, the responsibility to help the poor, and the importance of self-control in life. It's not about following rules but about changing hearts.

Praying the Stations of the Cross

For the last several years, I've made a weeklong pilgrimage to the Holy Land along with a group of pilgrims. Near the end of our time in Jerusalem, we walk the "Via Dolorosa," or "Way of the Cross," which traces the steps of Jesus from his condemnation by Pontius Pilate to his crucifixion. The locations of some stations are nearly certain (such as the location of Calvary, the hill on which Jesus was crucified). Others are less historical (such as the spots where Jesus fell).

In the 15th century, Christians in Europe began promoting the practice of praying with the stations in their local parishes because few could make the trip to the Holy Land.

So what might this ancient tradition say to you?

To begin with, it's not so important that every station is historical. (Veronica's wiping of Jesus' face is not even in the New Testament.) More important is the invitation to meditate on each of the stations, understanding that in their *totality* they are true—that is, Jesus was indeed condemned and tortured, suffered and was crucified. As you meditate, you might ask what each station means for you. For example: What does it mean to have someone help you carry your cross, as Simon of Cyrene did for Jesus? Are you open to letting someone share your suffering?

Each of the stations can open up a window into Jesus' life, and each can be a means for Jesus to enter your life, making holy any land you are in.

Praying in the Desert

It always surprises me how often the Gospels say that Jesus needed to "withdraw" from the crowds, and even the disciples, to pray. Like all of us, Jesus needed prayer, in his case, with the Father. And while the Gospels don't afford us much access to Jesus' inner life, we know that his prayer was real: that is, he truly sought help from the Father.

We also know that Jesus was really tempted. After his baptism, the Gospels describe Jesus as being "driven" or "led" into the desert for a period of testing. In Matthew and Luke we read the familiar incidents of Satan tempting Jesus in three ways: to turn stones into bread (to feed himself), to throw himself from a high tower (to prove God's loving care), and to worship Satan (in exchange for power and glory).

Like the most difficult temptations in our own lives, Jesus' temptations were cloaked in apparent goodness. Why wouldn't you want to feed yourself? Why not let God show you love? Why not acquire some wealth and power? The most tempting temptations rarely appear 100 percent evil, for then they would be easy to identify and reject. After much prayer, Jesus realized that giving into these lures would prevent him from becoming the person he was meant to be.

In the desert of our temptations, our lives can seem dry indeed. But if we follow the voice of conscience, and remember that God is always with us, we can, like Jesus, reject anything that leads us from becoming the flourishing person God wants us to be.

Praying with a Contrite Heart

In an interview for Jesuit magazines across the world in 2013, Pope Francis was asked to define himself. His first words in response were, "I am a sinner." Some people professed surprise that a pope would categorize himself as sinful, but for most Christians the response was probably, "So am I."

The Catholic Church has often been criticized for overemphasizing sin, for overwhelming people with guilt, and even for causing people to be ashamed of who they are. But lost in some of these critiques is an important truth: we are all indeed sinners. This is not to say that we are all unredeemed reprobates or terrible criminals; rather, we are all imperfect human beings who sin. Thus, a humble stance before God is natural.

Yet there is another equally important part of this equation. We are sinners—but we are loved passionately by God. That was the second part of Pope Francis's answer: "I am a sinner whom the Lord has looked upon." When praying, we must keep both realities in mind: we are sinful; we are loved.

Lent is a time of penance, and a time of prayer with a contrite heart. But it also is a time to pray with a heart that trusts in the love of God and hopes in the mercy of God.

If you doubt this, think about the Parable of the Prodigal Son, or the Parable of the Lost Sheep, or the Parable of the Lost Coin. God welcomes us, seeks us out, searches for us, sinners though we may be—and loves us all the while.

Easter Joy

Several years ago, during the Easter season, I was at Mass in a religious community. Before the Gospel was to be proclaimed, the priest walked to the ambo, looked down at the Lectionary, and said, with a grim expression on his face and in the flattest, most joyless voice imaginable, "Alleluia." In response, the group of ten people in the congregation responded, in a similarly flat and joyless voice, "Alleluia."

How can Easter be so ho-hum? Of course, as Christians we already know, even during Lent, that Christ is risen, so perhaps those joyless Alleluias reflect, paradoxically, the depth of our faith. If someone told you that the sun was going to rise tomorrow, your reaction would probably not be "How wonderful!" but "So what?"

But the emotions experienced by the disciples on the first Easter were far different. The Gospel writers use vivid words to convey, for example, the intense emotions of the women who receive news of Christ's resurrection. Mark uses the Greek word *ekthambeisthai* ("shocked and amazed") to describe how the women felt when they encountered two angels at the tomb. They then depart *tromos kai ekstasis* ("trembling and astonished"), the second word meaning "standing outside oneself." In other words, they are beside themselves. In Matthew, the women rush off with *phobou kai charas megalēs* ("fear and exceeding joy"). Christ's rising from the dead was the most dramatic event in history.

Let us never, ever, water down our Easter joy. Let our Alleluias be real. And loud. And, most of all, joyful.

Praying to the Risen Christ

What does it mean to pray to the Risen Christ? Let me suggest something that we often overlook: the Risen Christ is the same person he was before the resurrection. He is still Jesus of Nazareth, who walked the landscape of first-century Palestine, who spread the Good News and healed the sick, and who suffered and died. In other words, praying to the Risen Christ means praying to someone who is both fully divine *and* fully human, and who therefore understands your human struggles.

In one of Jesus' appearances to the disciples, he shows them "his hands and his side" (John 20:20). Why? First, to remind them that it is him. The Risen Christ is not some new person, someone other than the Jesus of Nazareth the disciples knew. His wounds are, as the New Testament scholar Stanley Marrow, SJ, said, his "credentials." They say, "It's me."

Second, his wounds show that Jesus still knows what it means to suffer. The Risen Christ carries within himself— or, more accurately, *on* himself—permanent reminders of his suffering. So when we pray to Christ, alive with the Father in heaven and present to us through the Spirit, we are praying not only to a divine Son but to a human being who still carries physical wounds on his body. To someone who knows what suffering means.

So the next time you pray to Jesus Christ, remember his wounds. And remember this: The Risen Christ remembers his human life because he is still human.

He understands you because he is still like you.

Neglect the Spirit No Longer

The Holy Spirit has often been called the forgotten member of the Trinity.

Many of us are in awe of the Father's handiwork in creation. When we cry out to "God," whether to express gratitude or ask for help, it is often the Father that we have in mind.

Perhaps even more of us feel that we have (or want to have) a close relationship with Jesus, the Second Person of the Trinity. We read about Jesus' preaching and healing in the Gospels, try to put his words into action, and celebrate the great milestones of his life during the liturgical year— from the Annunciation to the Ascension.

Not as many people have as strong a devotion to the Holy Spirit. This is surprising, because one could say that ever since Christ's time on earth came to a close, the Spirit is the primary way we experience God. Of course, theologically speaking, each person in the Trinity is present in the other, but it's still a fair statement: we experience God today, after Jesus' Ascension into heaven, mainly through the Spirit. Through our emotions, desires, insights, feelings, through our hopes and dreams, the Spirit encourages, consoles, and guides us.

So the next time you pray, why not direct your prayer to the Holy Spirit? Ask for the Spirit's guidance. Ask to notice where the Spirit is most active. Ask to have a felt awareness of the Spirit in your daily life. Neglect the Spirit no longer, for the Spirit never neglects you.

Visiting as Prayer

May is the month of the Visitation, the feast commemorating Mary's visit with Elizabeth after Mary discovers she is pregnant (Luke 1:39-56). The expectant mother rushes "with haste" to see her older relative. Why? Remember that Elizabeth herself is pregnant, with John the Baptist. So perhaps Mary realizes the elderly woman needs her help. Or perhaps Mary just wants to share her joy. Almost the first words out of her mouth are, "My soul magnifies the Lord!" Mary is the first proclaimer of the Good News: God is (almost) here!

While this passage might seem far from our experiences (miraculous pregnancies and the like), there are several invitations for reflection. To begin with, both Mary and Elizabeth take time to visit with one another, sharing not only friendship but stories of what God has done for them. This is one of the first recorded "spiritual conversations" in Christian history. How good it is to listen to our friends share how God is active in their lives. Sometimes when our faith feels weak, we can more easily see God at work in someone else. And this is a great help spiritually.

The Visitation also shows us the need to live more contemplatively. When I was working with refugees in East Africa, I often forgot to alter my normally rushed way of doing things. Once, during a hurried visit with a refugee, I checked my watch, and the refugee said sadly, "That's okay, Brother Jim. I know you are always in a hurry." Her comment reminded me of the call to spend time, to listen— and to visit.

Devoted Hearts

A mother once told me that when her son went away to college, "a part of my heart stepped into the world." I often think of her comment on the feasts of the Sacred Heart of Jesus and the Immaculate Heart of Mary.

Without getting into any complicated theological discussions, we can surely say that when Jesus left Nazareth to begin his public ministry, Mary must have felt that part of her heart went with him. And, as predicted earlier in the Gospel of Luke (2:35), her own heart was "pierced." That is, she would suffer when he did.

Devotion to the Sacred and Immaculate Hearts began in the Middle Ages and intensified in the 17th century. The visions of St. Margaret Mary Alacoque, a Visitation nun, and the subsequent preaching of her Jesuit spiritual director, St. Claude la Colombière, spread devotion to the Sacred Heart throughout Europe. At the same time, St. John Eudes, founder of the Congregation of Jesus and Mary, was highlighting interest in Mary's heart.

Some people are turned off by the kitschy images that attend both devotions. In some portrayals Jesus and Mary, with pale white faces and rouged cheeks, point to their hearts, which are depicted outside of their bodies. For those put off by those images, I like to ask simple questions to help them enter into these rich devotions: What would it mean for you to have a heart like Jesus? What would it mean for you to love like Mary?

More simply, what would it mean to have a part of God's heart in you, and out in the world?

Praying with Our Lady of Sorrows

I t's not accurate to say that the Blessed Mother led a sorrowful life. Hers was a fully human life, which means that she tasted the joys of being a mother, a wife, a daughter, a friend, as well as many other roles during her life in Nazareth that we can only guess at. Mary was, for example, probably the most esteemed member of the early Church, and her experiences clearly informed the writing of the Gospels.

But at times hers was also a sorrowful life. Near the beginning of the Gospel of Luke, a man named Simeon says to Mary, "A sword will pierce your own soul" (2:35). It's a dark prediction for Jesus' mother. And it comes true. Years later, Mary watches her sinless son die the most horrible death imaginable. Though she trusted in God and "treasured in her heart" her experiences at the Annunciation, she must have felt her soul "pierced" indeed.

This is why many are drawn to asking for the intercession of Our Lady of Sorrows, whose feast we celebrate on September 15. People understand that Mary, now in heaven, understands our grief. She understands our confusion as well. While she remembered the Annunciation, and was present at her son's first miracle at Cana, she must have been overwhelmed by confusion and frustration as Jesus died on the Cross.

Yet Mary understands something else—with God, death is never the last word. For Our Lady of Sorrows also experienced the Risen Lord and, at that moment, became Our Lady of Joys.

November: Not Downbeat at All

Does saying that November is the month of the dead sound downbeat? It shouldn't, because the two feast days at the beginning of the month, which set the tone for the next twenty-eight days, are about God's mercy and love.

All Saints Day (November 1) is perhaps better understood. On that day Catholics celebrate those who have gained entrance into heaven. That means all the saints—known and unknown—not just the ones who are officially canonized. These are the men, women, and children who availed themselves fully of God's love on earth.

On All Souls Day (November 2) we remember the "faithful departed," those who have died but are still in purgatory. Purgatory has always made sense to me. Few of us are ready to meet God when we die, and so we may need to go through a process of preparation to ready our souls to encounter the Living God. And those in the midst of this preparation need our loving support. You pray for someone after their death just as you would pray for someone on earth going through a difficult trial.

How can you pray for the dead? Besides having Masses celebrated in memory of a loved one, you can do something as simple as calling to mind their faces and asking God to forgive their sins. Or you can pray a Rosary, or any sort of familiar prayer, as a way of showing your love and asking for God's mercy. In the fullness of time, we pray that all of us will be gathered together, where we will rejoice in God's merciful love.

And that's not downbeat at all, is it?

Grieving in Prayer

November is a time when Catholics remember the "faithful departed," those souls who are still in purgatory and, more broadly, all those who have gone before us. During this month, then, I often think about what it means to grieve in prayer.

Even devout believers sometimes feel uncomfortable expressing sadness in prayer. They may feel that it is somehow ungrateful. But, as in any relationship, if a person expresses only the feelings he or she thinks they "should" express, the relationship grows cold.

God desires for us to be ourselves in prayer, and that includes being honest when we are mourning the death of a loved one, experiencing sadness over failures, or dealing with loss as we transition to a new stage of life.

One way to grieve in prayer is to imagine sitting with Jesus. Remember that Jesus himself knew true sadness and real loss. Of course his greatest grief came at the crucifixion, when his disciples abandoned him and he had to accept what looked like an apparent end to his great project. But earlier in life, Jesus most likely wept over many things, including the death of St. Joseph, who, significantly, is not present at the crucifixion.

Imagine yourself sitting with Jesus, and share your grief with one who understands these emotions. If you feel comfortable, you might imagine Jesus speaking to you about loss.

In this way you may feel a deeper union with the God who grieves alongside us.

Afterword

As I mentioned in the introduction, even after Jesus taught his disciples to pray the Our Father, they still had more to learn about prayer. After all, the disciples were human. That meant that for the rest of their lives, they probably both struggled with prayer, sometimes finding it dry, and enjoyed prayer, sometimes finding it filled with consolation.

After Jesus' time on earth had ended and the disciples were charged with spreading the Gospel, the early Christians probably said to them, "Teach us to pray."

We can always ask God to teach us to pray. For prayer is not something we learn once and for all. And I don't think we ever "master" it. In my own life, I'm always discovering new practices and insights, and try to remain open to whatever God wants to reveal to me about prayer.

I hope that this short book has helped you a bit in your own life of prayer. Most of all, I hope that it's helped you to draw closer to God, who wants to be ever closer to you, in your daily life and in your prayer.

Acknowledgments

I would like to thank Mary Stommes, Peter Dwyer, and Ælred Senna, OSB, of Liturgical Press for inviting me to contribute the "Teach Us to Pray" monthly column to *Give Us This Day* several years ago. Thanks to Mary and Peter for suggesting that these essays might become a book, and a special thanks to Mary for collecting, editing, and organizing the selections into helpful chapters.

And, of course, thanks to God, who makes all things possible.

This work was typeset in Minion Pro on Apple Macintosh.

Design by Ann Blattner with interior art by Frank Kacmarcik, OblSB.

Printed by Versa Press, Inc.

Also available from *Give Us This Day* Books:

Blessed Among Us
Day by Day with Saintly Witnesses
by Robert Ellsberg

Hardcover, ribbon, 792 pp
$29.95   978-0-8146-4721-9
eBook $19.99   978-0-8146-4745-5
www.litpress.org
800-858-5450

". . . challenges us to widen our understanding of holiness and sainthood, and to open our eyes to the 'saints' around us today."
            —Sebastian Gomes, *Subject Matters*, Salt + Light TV

The Work of Your Hands
*Prayers for Ordinary and
Extraordinary Moments of Grace*
by Diana Macalintal

Paperback, 80 pp
$7.95   978-0-8146-3803-3
www.litpress.org
800-858-5450

". . . full of comforting, wise, and useful words, that will console and enliven you, and help you do the same for others."
            —Fran Rossi Szpylczyn, *There Will Be Bread* at
            breadhere.wordpress.com

ThisGive Us**Day**®

These essays on prayer by James Martin, SJ,
are drawn from the "Teach Us to Pray" column in
Give Us This Day, a personal daily prayer book
published monthly by Liturgical Press.

For more information or to request a sample copy
of *Give Us This Day*, go to www.gutd.net
or call 888-259-8470.